Citizens Vote in a Democracy

Nancy Anderson

Rosen REAL READERS

Rosen Classroom™
New York

Here I am with my mom and dad. We live in Vermont. We are citizens of the United States.

Citizens of the United States live in a **democracy**. "Democracy" means "rule by the people." This means that citizens have a say in the government.

Citizens in the United States pick whom they want their leaders to be. They vote for candidates in an **election.**

In the United States, any **citizen** over 18 can vote in an election. They can vote for whomever they want. It is their choice.

Our town is having an election. The election is to decide who will be the next mayor. The person who gets the most votes wins the election.

Each candidate gives a speech. They say what they want for the town. They say how they will make the town a better place.

My mother hopes Mr. Johnson wins the election. He wants to build a new park. This park will have an area to plant fruits and vegetables.

My father wants Ms. Edwards to win the election. Ms. Edwards wants to build a new ice-skating rink. Hockey games will be played on the rink.

My parents go to the **municipal center** to vote. They go in the voting booth. The ballot has four names. My parents vote for the candidate they want to win.

A machine counts the votes.

Mr. Johnson wins! He will be the new mayor of our town!

Glossary

citizen A person who legally belongs to a country.

democracy A political system in which people pick whom their leaders will be.

election The act of selecting or voting for someone or something.

municipal center A city or town hall.